Charlemagne's Rivers
Nick Monks

Bluebell Publishing

For Amanda, Karl, Saskia

By the same author

Poetry

By the Canal (Masque Publishing)
Winter Trees
Cities Like Jerusalem
Homes
The Love Songs of James Dyer
Narratives
Gardening
Imaginary Friends
England's of the Mind
Snow
Greek Olympian Myth
Footprints (The Disparate)

Plays

Le Conquet (The Refugees)

Short stories

Aegean Islands

Title Page

Charlemagne's Rivers- Nick Monks

Copyright © 2019 by Nick Monks

Published by Bluebell Publishing- November 2019

Printed by Lulu
www.lulu.com

ISBN:.978-0-9569386-8-8

CONTENTS

Greek Mountains   9

Fishermen, Eilat, Israel   10

Lappeenranta- Finland   11

Le Conquet- Bretagne, France   12

Ashdot Ya'akou Meuhad- Kibbutz – Israel   13

Brighton   14

Berlin   16

Beppu, Kyushu, Japan   18

Lake Toba, Sumatra, Indonesia   20

Blue Hotel- Paris   21

New York   22

Delft, Holland   23

Frieberg, Germany   24

Myrdal, Norway   25

Malacca, Malaysia   27

Morocco   28

Copenhagen   29

Tiberius, Israel   30

Menorca, Spain   31

Portugal   32

Willesden Green, London   33

Istanbul   34

Aswan, Egypt   35

Chang Mai, Thailand   36

Eilat, Negev Desert, Israel   37

Credo   38

Charlemagne's Rivers

Greek Mountains

The hitched lift took you north
The driver informed you he was veering off the route

There were two roads
You chose to walk into a forest
After five miles
A sign said "Albanian border 2 kilometres" ahead

So- you walked back to the second road
Walked along the narrow lane higher
Into the Pindus mountains
It is spring and alpine flowers bloom
A herd of deer fleet across the mountain meadow

In a tiny village you have the worst tasting soup
You have ever tasted
You ask by sign language can you sleep on the café veranda
The lady says yes
While you sleep fireflies dance in the night.

Fisherman, Eilat

From the sand
The nets spread out into the Red sea
Seven of you have been hired
As fishermen
Two go out in a boat to prepare the nets
You and others pull in the nets
In the shallows are a shoal of caught small tuna
You paddle
Scoop out the fish, five dangling
By tail fin from your fingers
And put them in crates
You don't like killing fish
The sun cascades in warmth on your skin.

Lappeenranta- Finland

The hotel is expensive
You go out into the town
Then by the lake
The Finnish are enjoying their weekend
In groups in restaurants and customers of weekend kiosks
You buy an ice cream
Walk along lake Saimaa shore
Past the people gathered in crowds
Further on
Around the vast lakes shore
Until you are alone
With little auk, middle spotted woodpecker, skua
These faultless beings by the empty silver lake.

Le Conquet, Bretagne, France

You camp at Camping Les Blancs Sablons
Walk over the dunes
A beautiful white sand beach with waves crashing
From the tumultuous deep blue/green Atlantic
At night you walk into the town
For a restaurant pizza
Glow worm's, white dots of light in the heath
In the morning an elderly lady you befriended
Arrives with breakfast in a Tupperware box

You want to stay for weeks to write that novel
That always seems the wrong time to start
From your study/office
A dark green two- man tent below the tree boughs
Opposite the library of the Atlantic sea/sky horizon.

Ashdot Ya'akov Meuhad, Kibbutz- Israel

In the cinema you watch a film
About Amadeus Mozart
You are tired with *"partying" "drinking"*
After an ill- advised citrus throwing contest/war
You read *My Life* by Golda Meir
And *Thief's in the Night* by Arthur Koestler
And one of the *Alexandria Quartet* by Lawrence Durrell
On the accommodation veranda

After work- avocado, banana, orange or grapefruit harvesting.
Or working on the date plantation or factory or kitchen work-

You go for long walks or light jogs
Along the Jordan/ Israeli border
Razor wire, landmines, the river Jordan
Until the army tell you, you are not allowed
As there may be snipers on the Jordanian side

There are though other routes and walks

Except for the details of daily routine
This is all that happens
Work, reading, walks
Bulbuls, Palestine Sunbird, White Throated Kingfisher-
Amos Oz/ Andre Brink/ Lawrence Durrell
And the thousands of details and anecdotes-
That remain life not art.

Brighton

The B and B room is surprisingly comfortable
Craig has been thrown out of his flat
And has moved in on your recommendation
So- evenings of loud music and hash

You work two shifts at Wheelie hotel
Washing and drying plates, cutlery, pans
Finishing the second shift at 1 am

When there is time you wander the lanes of Brighton
Listening to Thomson Twins or the Cure or Elkie Brooks
On the Walkman. Gazing out at the English Channel
Buffeted in darkness by the wind

One week three letters arrive:

One from Karen …. "You seem to forget, I'm studying in
Brighton…. I suggest we meet….."

One from Hull University…. "You have been accepted to study
philosophy, the three- year coarse starts on 15th October."

One from Project 67…… "Your application has been processed
and the flight will depart from Gatwick on the 8th of November…
you will be allocated to a kibbutz on arrival in Tel Aviv."

You wander in the gale along Grand Parade, the Royal Pavilion,
the Lanes

Sit on a sea wall. As the Cure sing- *The Forest* and the Thomson Twins- *Storm on the Sea.*

Berlin

For three days you stand in phone booths
But you parents have disabled their phone

Finally you march down the Strabe des 17. Juni
Past the Russian tank. Through the Brandenburg gate
To the British embassy and demand to see the ambassador

You have been to the post office every day for four weeks
In Berlin Zoo
But no metformin for diabetes has arrived
Finally speaking in English for the first time in four weeks
They tell you "Berlin post only do post restante for letters"

To kill time you visit the Olympic stadium three times
Hitler's bunker three times. Check point Charlie six times
Charlottenburg Palace three times.
The last sections of the Berlin wall 10 times.
You see Brecht's flat in East Berlin and visit his
And Fichte (the philosopher, who inverted Hegel's dialectic)
And the poet Becker's grave
And know the forests and parks around Berlin extremely well

The ambassador makes phone calls for you
But ambassadors have no sway with your parents
You ring aunts, childhood friends,
Then a solicitor friend who sends you £300
You have been in Berlin camping for 6 weeks
Waiting for metformin so you can stay with Anna in Warsaw

You loose £150. Somebody steals your bag in a shop.
You now have no passport.
Your suffering withdrawal symptoms,
And your blood sugars could be way to high
In an attempt to get metformin you see an official in charge
Of bilateral medical care who tells you "the British never pay"
And directs you five miles to a mental health ward who luckily let
you go (without metformin)
You ring up the consulate a woman who's out socializing says
"Why didn't you stay on that ward Gerta sent you to"

A para- military with machine gun calls you sir and ushers
You in to see the ambassador for the fourth time
He has printed your passport finds out that a coach to London
from Berlin is £110, you have £120
At Berlin Zoo you are first frantically on the coach
A pretty blonde woman asks can she sit next to you
She says she was watching me and couldn't place me
What liberal tolerant people the Germans are you think.

Beppu-Kyushu, Japan

I came from Kyoto's gardens and Osaka's traffic, Mount Fuji.
The green mountains taste like sweet, sunless, damp moss,
the sort of blue Rothko paints, the sea, a Gaugin sky.
Fishing boats and nets, lobster pots, harbour walls.

The hotel would only let me check in, the room was available at 2pm,
as is the custom in Japanese hotels,
so I wandered the small town for four hours disconsolate, hurt even.
Tried to climb one of the mountains, but couldn't: got sunburnt,

Asked the sea why I was always alone and was this good or not,
To which she answered truthfully your not.
So I am now thirsty in the middle of Beppu, adding up objects to try and make infinity.

Elsewhere I count three Stars of David on arty Christmas trees;
In the thirty visits to the park
Eight benches, two Mc Donald's, five pretty women, eighty cars.

Christmas day was a day of aloneness,
a quiet and peace that tenuously vibrated in the air-
a sort of not- Christmas, that made it more so.
A pleasurable Christmas.

Now, having a room in a town of fishermen and Christmas lights,
A place of conditioned cool air and a stillness without clocks

Trying to climb mountains of syntax and logical equations with mere, small love.

Lake Toba, Sumatra, Indonesia

At the bus station
Twelve people gather around you
In a circle
Trying to sell you mosquito net, bus ticket, cigarettes and other

The lake is vast
On the boat you wish for aloneness
The volcano centre island nears
You pass on the first 5 landing jetties

Choose the sixth
And check into a smart cheap hotel
There are five hotel staff
One guest only, you

You make a half attempt to, walk into, explore the island
But are deterred by packs of "stray" dogs
So spend four days at the hotel
With your five servants
Gazing out each day across the silver lake

When you announce you are leaving
The manager expresses his regret and disappointment.

Blue Hotel, Paris

The neon sign rattled in the wind
"HOTEL" in bright red. The front door was tired
The lobby dull in lead grey tones
Sheen of rain- water, sagging beds, seedy dregs of the city

I came from another place and time
To insomnia and broken loves and promises
I head out reluctantly to Panini stalls, neon, granite, rain
At night the lead pipe- work gulped and chimed and clinked

The room seemed to get greyer
The stairs where strewn with rotting apples
A blue tit sat on the table, pecked at my sleeping eyelids
I bandaged my head with a shredded shirt

So I went to another Hotel, then another, then another
In one of the world's greatest decaying cities
After three weeks, I sat on the banks of the Seine canal
(not the river Seine) and looked into nothing

Saw a seagull, flap on wet November air
Looked at a map, a timetable, checked, rechecked
Worked out the route back, the ticket in hand
To a suburban door in glossy white called HOME

New York

You have 24 hours till your flight
Been to Los Angeles, Mexico, San Francisco, Pittsburgh
So you set out to walk to Manhattan from JFK
Except its 23 km and you don't know the route
Your given a lift, by chance

Drive through central park
See where Blondie, Patti Smith, The New York Dolls, Sex Pistols,
played
Get out of the car look at the statue of liberty
Have lunch pasta and wine in an Italian restaurant
Visit a strip joint
He's from the Dominican Republic works on Wall Street, he says
"I can't wait to tell my wife what a great guy I met"
See Broadway then Times Square
Drive along Maddison avenue looking at "well shod people"
Then he drives you back to JFK
What a swell guy you think
As you ponder the surly folks of Yorkshire, Hull awaiting you.

Delft, Holland

You arrive
The town centre is picturesque
You know no one here
Have no relatives
Friends
Never heard of Delft
Before you opened your lonely planet in Rotterdam
So Delft is the thump of home
You have longed for all your life
Your rustic antique town centre streets
Your majestic green canals
The milling people lover's mortal enemies colleagues
Childhood friends
The town you grew up in
And therefore you must leave your life long home
And go into a one- thousand- year exile
A diaspora spanning the world
But one day your great, great, great, great predecessors will return
Once again embracing the green canals
Treading over the cobbled cankered streets
Falling in love again.

Frieberg, Germany

At the camp site
You take advantage of the wide spaces
And camp away from the others
Right by the bank of the lake
Leaving just enough of room to
Leave and enter the tent
You make forays into the city
Climb black forest hills
Loiter in the enchanted forests

For two weeks
When you return
The lake has changed its colour each time
Silver, blue, purple, red
To welcome you a bereft tramp
Back to centre of your becoming.

Myrdal, Norway

The city of Myrdal comprises
A café, a ticket office, a toilet, a waiting room
To escape the teeming city
Your walk past the youngsters
Throwing snow at each other
Ascend into the high valley of the Hardangervidda
Until the slope rises to steep to ascend
And ahead are sheer cliffs
There is no route onto the plateau via here
Serenaded by an arctic fox, snow grouse, lemmings

The arctic fox paws regally away treading the slope you can't
climb
Lemmings stand in front of you and shake, purr/growling
Then run away at about two feet distance
The snow grouse stand imperially on a prominent rock
Then aflight on your approach

Back, you catch the mountain train to Flam
The tannoy says
"The tunnel where in turns 180 degrees
 Was built over five years
At night to avoid being seen or heard by the occupying Nazis"
On the other side of the tunnel
The train stops
You get out onto a wooden platform
A forceful river with segmented water underneath

Traditional Norwegian music plays
A mountain maid appears waves
Then further away another appears waves
Then disappears behind a rock

In Flam you buy supermarket food
Check in at a campsite
Sit by the fjord in a cafe sipping cappuccino
While other types of animals and creatures pass

Why didn't I follow, thus the world was born
The mountains – calling.

Malacca, Malaysia

You left Hat Yai
After sleeping with Yasmin
The fierce storm in your head is still unabated

The girl on the bus in Muslim Malaysia
Politely replies to your conversation
Then stands at her embarkation
And says "you can still walk"

In Malacca you follow routine
And seek out the Chinese quarter to lodge
It is so peaceful after Kuala Lumpur
As you run
Into the fierce night, the cicadas, dry violins
Of a new world.

Morocco

The boat to Tangiers
The girl at the till selling cigarettes
The dusty white town
Of white stucco houses
You have come
To swim into the Sahara desert
A frontier town
The insignificance of the Atlas Mountains
Now dive-

Copenhagen

The city was pretty enough
Spacious squares-with orange, green and red ornate buildings

After km's of walking
Shedding skin and people
There was Hans Christian Andersons mermaid sculpture
By the shore
Engulphed by this human tragedy
Longing to return to the sea
Yet cheat death
Undo the spell,
Become the purity
Of a mythical before.

Tiberius, Israel

Sun dappled
Wine soaked, olive scented oils
Cool white plaster shade
Thousands of dark noble life's
Hidden behind lattice balconies

Dreams becoming day healed
Free from abrasion

The lake a silver chalice of blue ice
That comes
Into the doorways and eyes of the blind
The beggar the kings and princes

As the sky sheets
The Golan heights far away across the silver and gold lake

Menorca, Spain

The swished return and repost and return
Of table tennis
The heavy petting with Tina
The comic dives from the swimming pool diving board
The film you saw
Glasses of iced soft drinks in the bar
The inter-hotels football match
Fishing for octopus with water spear off the shore

Walking away into the Mediterranean woods
Through the pine and prickly pear scent
You know where you are going
Into a world away from or to just keep walking
Derrida, Francois Lyotard, Saussure, Baudrillard
Or Avalon truffles in the arid parched soil
Of the Mediterranean coastal pine forest.

Portugal

In Covilha after a night in a hotel
You scour the map
There is an off- road route up Torre (Serra da Estrela)
But you climb via the steep winding road
No one gives you a lift though
At half ascent a stray dog joins you
You don't know why
She treads in front of you
As if a family pet of 7 years
At the summit some snow
You buy a coke and drink
In the tourist retail centre
Gaze at the view with your family pet
The dog stays outside the train carriage in Covilha
As you travel back to Lisbon

For the last five years
You imagine you, Emily, two kids
Putting ceremonially on a dog collar
Opening the back of the Volvo
Quiet words at Dover port to an official

The farm you, Emily, two kids
Bracken in the farm courtyard
You the stray at home in the cold September air
The swallows on the wires, the hay in
Frost shards on the farm window- panes, the fields stretching.

Willesden Green- London

You were given the address by a friend
The B and B- room has three beds
Usually there's just the two of you

The Irish tinker disappears for days
After DWP pay day
He returns at 4am one day
Drunk with a badly bruised face
And abrasions to his hands
He threatens to smash his whisky bottle over you
When you ask him to stop singing
So you sleep that night in the dining room

You work 12 hours a day in a Macdonald's on the Strand
Commute by tube there
Often walk back as you've missed the 00.05 last train
On your day off
You jog to and on Hampstead Heath
Sitting looking out over this great and debauched city.

Istanbul

Mapping a new city
Every time you enter or leave the hotel
The staff try to sell you tours
You acquiesce enjoying the conversation

Half of an historian
You wander this gateway city
The Muslim mind impervious to Rome

In Saint Sofia the monks merged into the wall
When the Muslims took back Constantinople
One day they may re- emerge. So the story goes

You do not feel at ease here
In the hotel you listen to the tour offers
Glance at the brochures. Say "you'll think about it"
Visit the blue mosque, stand on the banks of the Bosporus
Hail a taxi- and say…. "airport please."

Aswan, Egypt

The group your with
Comprises two Swedish girls
Two Norwegian men, and another Englishman

You love the overladen heat
The tall blacks in brightly coloured cloths
Cairo didn't seem like Africa
Aswan does

On the Aswan dam built by the Russians
You look down the sheer curved colossal sides
But really you are looking at the vast lake
Really gazing south
Where like Grahame Greens- *The Heart of the Matter*
Or Conrad's- *Heart of Darkness*
You shall be utterly healed by Africa-
Like Golda Meir. Or other intrepid's have been before.

Chang Mai, Thailand

You wander the city
Past esoteric Buddhist temples
You know little about
Skirt the wall fortress of the old city
The girl in the café you go to everyday
Is not for you

North, the hotel is chalets in spacious grounds
A hotel worker drives you in his car
To the rain forest
That seems to you as pastoral as the New Forest
Or Grizedale or the forests of the Black Forest

Past elephants and rice paddocks
You buy a plate and jug from the Karen
The tribes earn money conglomerating in this village

Back at the hotel disappointed
You watch tv with Yasmin and forget
And remember about the café girl in Chang Mai.

Eilat, Negev Desert, Israel

In Eilat Israel working for 7 months
You dream every day of walking
Into the Negev/Sinai desert
Thirty- two years later you realize
This in a poem

You tread/ skeletons is it/ bone/
Marry the sun/ delicious heat

Dry waddis/ a rare glimpse of a leopard/ then a Sooty falcon
A sharp high mountain ridge/ surrounded by migrating honey
buzzards/ close almost touching
Your wings/ there wings/ your wings

Bequeathed three colours amber sand/ blue sky/ the azure red
sea/ thirst/ exhaustion/ foot fall into foot fall
Over the razor wire and landmines from the Negev to Sinai/
seamless desert/everywhere sun-crash

I am dying/ purple lightning/ rain torrent/ vultures circling/ arid
hallucinations/ sun beckoning death

Away with the Bedouin caravan/ twelve years plying trade routes
in the Negev/Sinai/Sahara/the stars crystal clear blooms/ camels
eating fodder/ Turkish tea around the desert fire.

The grieving that can only be healed by the sight of Jerusalem.

Credo

In a room I never venture out from
Listening to the Atlantic storms on the windowpane
Sitting in the deep freezer
Relishing the coldness of tap water
The polar bear and wolverine run away
As I write of the verdant bounteous cities
Toying with the allure of places not visited.

www.ingramcontent.com/pod-product-compliance
Lightning Source LLC
Chambersburg PA
CBHW031336040426
42443CB00005B/365